WITHDRAWAL

**AVAILABLE NOW
from Lerner Publishing Services!**

The *On the Hardwood* series:

Boston Celtics	Miami Heat
Brooklyn Nets	Minnesota Timberwolves
Chicago Bulls	New York Knicks
Dallas Mavericks	Oklahoma City Thunder
Houston Rockets	Philadelphia 76ers
Indiana Pacers	Portland Trail Blazers
Los Angeles Clippers	San Antonio Spurs
Los Angeles Lakers	Utah Jazz

COMING SOON!

Additional titles in
the *On the Hardwood* series:

Atlanta Hawks
Cleveland Cavaliers
Denver Nuggets
Detroit Pistons
Golden State Warriors
Memphis Grizzlies
Phoenix Suns
Washington Wizards

To Order • www.lernerbooks.com • 800-328-4929 • fax 800-332-1132

ON THE HARDWOOD

HOUSTON ROCKETS

RON BERMAN

On the Hardwood: Houston Rockets

MVP Books
2255 Calle Clara
La Jolla, CA 92037

MVP Books is an imprint of Book Buddy Digital Media, Inc., 42982 Osgood Road, Fremont, CA 94539

MVP Books publications may be purchased for
educational, business, or sales promotional use.

Cover and layout design by Jana Ramsay
Copyedited by Susan Sylvia
Photos by Getty Images

ISBN: 978-1-61570-853-6 (Library Binding)
ISBN: 978-1-61570-837-6 (Soft Cover)

TABLE OF CONTENTS

Chapter 1
TWIN TOWERS

Basketball is popular all around the world, and there are NBA fans almost everywhere you go. Some of the best fans you'll ever find live in the Lone Star State. As the saying goes, "Everything is bigger in Texas." That may be why there are three NBA teams there. Each one of them, the Rockets, Spurs, and Mavericks, have experienced the joy of winning a championship.

The Rockets were actually the first team in Texas, even before the Mavericks and Spurs. However, many young fans may not know that the Rockets actually got their start in San Diego, California. The franchise was born there in 1967. The team was named the Rockets in honor of the fact that San Diego was building rockets for the National Aeronautics and Space Administration (more commonly referred to as NASA).

Many significant things happened in the early days of the franchise. Two of them actually happened on the day of the 1970 NBA draft. The Rockets held two picks: the second pick overall, and

The San Diego Rockets tip off against the New York Knicks in a 1970 game.

also the first pick of the second round.

With their first selection, the Rockets went for a small forward from the University of Michigan. He would end up becoming a five-time All-Star—and more importantly,

Calvin Murphy and Rudy Tomjanovich.

one of the most beloved coaches in the history of the organization. His name was Rudy Tomjanovich.

With their second pick, the Rockets found a player who would turn into an All-Star and a future Hall of Famer. Even though Calvin Murphy was only 5'9" tall, that didn't stop him from averaging 18 points a game over his outstanding 13-year career.

In 1971, the San Diego Rockets moved to Texas and became the Houston Rockets. For the next 10 years, they were a successful and competitive team. Besides Tomjanovich and Murphy, they also had Moses Malone, one of the greatest centers in NBA history. Malone, a three-time Most Valuable Player, was inducted into the NBA

Hall of Fame in 2001. He led the Rockets all the way to the NBA Finals in 1981.

Two short years later, everything had changed for the Houston Rockets. Moses Malone was traded to Philadelphia, signaling a rebuilding effort on the part of the Rockets. The memory of the 1981 march to the NBA Finals faded quickly as the Rockets won only 14 games and became a lottery team. As most fans know, the NBA "lottery" is reserved for teams that don't make the playoffs. It's like when friends draw sticks or flip a coin to see who gets to choose something first. In the NBA, the lottery is a way of determining the order in which teams will select in the draft. The Rockets won the

Moses Malone was unstoppable around the rim.

lottery, which entitled them to the first pick of the 1983 draft.

When draft day arrived, there was no suspense. Everyone knew who the Rockets would select:

Media Exposure
By the time Ralph Sampson became a Rocket, he had already appeared on the cover of Sports Illustrated five times!

Ralph Sampson, one of the most well-known and anticipated college prospects in many years. He was a center, but he played with the skill of a guard. He was a versatile and athletic big man who truly had all the tools.

Ralph had always been a big kid. When you're in middle school, there's always somebody who's much taller than everybody else. But when was the last time you saw a ninth grader who was 6'7" tall? That was Ralph Sampson. And he was still growing. By the time he graduated from high school and was preparing to attend the University of Virginia, he was almost 7'4" tall.

In his first season with the Houston Rockets, Sampson did not disappoint. This young phenom averaged 21 points and 11 rebounds. Still, the NBA is a team game. One great player isn't enough to have a successful season. Although the Rockets showed improvement, mainly because of Sampson, they still finished with a record of only 29-53.

Fans in Houston had great reason for optimism. Just like the year before, the Rockets held the number one pick in the draft. Luckily they didn't have to look too far to find their man.

While the Rockets had been struggling the past couple of years, things were completely different at the nearby University of Houston. The Cougars had standout years in 1983 and 1984. The main reason was their athletic seven-foot center. His name was Hakeem Olajuwon.

Olajuwon was born in Lagos, Nigeria in 1963. He lived near a very

Late Bloomer

Incredibly, Hakeem didn't even start playing basketball until the age of 15.

large field, where he and his friends played soccer every day. Basketball wouldn't come until much later— but meanwhile, Hakeem was developing the athleticism and dexterity that would become his hallmark on the basketball court.

In the 1984 draft, the Rockets selected Olajuwon because they wanted to pair him with Ralph Sampson. The idea was to move the versatile Sampson over to power forward, with Olajuwon playing center. It didn't take long for the "Twin Towers" to become a major force in the NBA.

In the 1985-86 season, the Rockets won 51 games and charged

Towering Success

In the 1985-86 season, both Olajuwon and Sampson averaged double-doubles (double figures in points and rebounds).

into the playoffs. They went head-to-head with the defending champion Los Angeles Lakers in the Western Conference Finals. The Rockets stormed out to a three-games-to-one lead—before the epic conclusion to Game 5.

With only one second left in Game 5, the score was tied at 112. After a timeout, the Rockets inbounded the ball from half-court.

Rodney McRae spotted Ralph Sampson, who was stationed just below the free-throw line. With only one second to go, Sampson wouldn't have time to gather himself, turn, and shoot. So instead, he jumped into the air to receive the pass. Then, all in one motion, Sampson twisted his body while still in midair, and threw the ball toward the rim. The buzzer sounded as the ball danced on the rim and then softly dropped straight through.

It was virtually impossible to get around, over, or through the Twin Towers.

The 1980s Rockets were a loose, fun group...they even recorded a rap song, which became a hit in Houston!

The Lakers and their fans were so stunned they couldn't believe it. Maybe the Rockets didn't believe it either for a moment. But as soon as they realized that they had won the game and eliminated the Lakers, they jumped in the air with joy. Three years earlier they had been a lottery team. Now they were going to the NBA Finals!

Even though the Rockets lost in the NBA Finals to the Boston Celtics, it had been a magical year. Their future looked bright and they figured that it wouldn't be long before *they* would be the ones holding up the championship trophy. Unfortunately it didn't happen quite as fast as Rockets fans hoped. In fact, it would take close to 10 years. But memorable things are sometimes worth waiting for, as the Rockets and their fans would eventually find out.

Chapter 2
LAYING THE FOUNDATION

Sadly, the promise and potential of the Twin Towers was never realized. Injuries were the main reason, especially for Ralph Sampson. Because of knee and back issues, the great big man was never the same. Within a couple of years he had been traded to the Golden State Warriors.

Many Houston fans became discouraged. The Rockets seemed to be heading in the wrong direction. From 1988 to 1991, they lost in the first round of the playoffs each year. Then, in 1992, they didn't even make the playoffs. Nobody could have blamed fans for losing hope.

Luckily, the Rockets still had Hakeem Olajuwon. Year after year, he was putting up All-Star numbers. His signature move was the famous "Dream Shake." Utilizing the footwork he had developed on the soccer field, Hakeem consistently faked out his opponents with a series of clever moves. He could go

With his vast array of moves, Hakeem was very difficult to guard.

Otis Thorpe was the perfect power forward to play alongside Hakeem.

left or right, and the end result was usually two points.

Hakeem couldn't do it all by himself, though. He needed help, and luckily help was on the way. In 1988, the Rockets pulled off a big trade which netted them power forward Otis Thorpe. At the time, Thorpe was only in his fifth year. He was coming off a season in which he had been one of only five players who had averaged 20 points and 10 rebounds. It was clear that he would be the perfect complement to Olajuwon. The first big piece of the puzzle was in place.

A couple of years later, in 1990, the Rockets acquired guard Kenny Smith in a trade with the Atlanta Hawks. Many fans know Kenny from his work on NBA TV, as well as pregame and post-game analyst on TNT. It's always been fun to watch him joke around and mix it up with Charles Barkley. But long before the funny stuff, Kenny was a lightning-quick guard who could beat players off the dribble and also knock down three-pointers.

Then there was Vernon Maxwell, AKA "Mad Max." He was a fearless competitor and a very talented player. Maxwell, a 6'4" guard, played with great passion, and his skills were undeniable. Once, in a 1991 regular-season game, he led the Rockets past the Cleveland Cavaliers with one of the most remarkable performances in Rockets history. He scored 51 incredible

Cry Me a River
Smith has made many good-natured excuses about it, but he provided many laughs in a celebrity All-Star game once…when Justin Timberlake hit a jumper over him and started trash-talking!

points—including 30 points in the fourth quarter alone!

The athletic Vernon Maxwell scores on a beautiful driving layup.

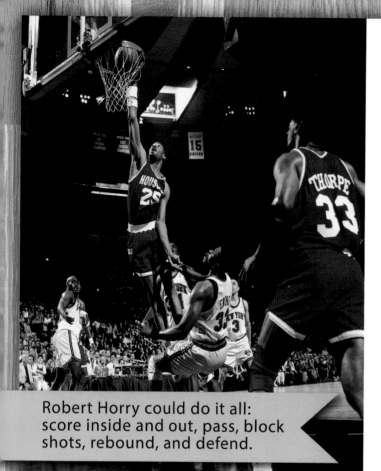

Robert Horry could do it all: score inside and out, pass, block shots, rebound, and defend.

of the greatest clutch players in NBA history. Maybe that's why he ended up winning seven championships in his career. That's more than Larry Bird, Magic Johnson, Michael Jordan, Kobe Bryant, Shaquille O'Neal and LeBron James—as a matter of fact, in the last forty years, no NBA player has more championship rings than Robert Horry!

A couple years later, in the 1992 NBA draft, the Rockets drafted 6'10" Robert Horry from the University of Alabama. Horry was a skilled defender, an excellent shot blocker, and a threat from three-point range. Known for being cool under fire, he would go on to be regarded as one

The Rockets were making progress. In 1993 they advanced beyond the first round of the play-offs for the first time in six years. They ended up losing a seven-game series to the Seattle SuperSonics in the semifinals of the Western Conference playoffs. Although it was a tough loss, things were clearly moving in the right direction.

The transformation of the Houston Rockets was nearly complete. In the 1993 draft, the Rockets held the 24th pick. They used it to select a dynamic scoring guard named Sam Cassell. In his senior year at Florida State, Cassell had averaged 18 points a game. His leadership and strong play had helped the Seminoles march all the way to the Elite Eight of the NCAA tournament. This was a sign of good things to come for the future NBA All-Star. Over the course of his terrific career, the 6'3" guard would go on to score more than 15,000 points and

Having Fun
The Rockets ended up with a very talented and colorful cast of characters. One of them was the uncontrollable Sam Cassell. He wasn't shy on—or off—the court!

distribute more than 5,000 assists.

In the summer of 1993, the Rockets found themselves with a new owner. Leslie Alexander purchased the team and immediately

Cassell beats his man off the dribble and prepares to set up a teammate for an easy layup.

Mario Elie, affectionately called "Junkyard Dog," was a tough and aggressive player.

as a defensive stopper. His three-point shooting was also steadily improving. This would prove to be very important for the Rockets. The popular Elie had some cool nicknames, including "Super Mario" (a reference to the videogame Super Mario Brothers).

Between 1988 and 1993, the Rockets underwent so many changes that it was hard to keep track. They had a new owner, many new players, and even a new leader, as former Rockets great Rudy Tomjanovich took over as head coach. However, they still had the great Hakeem Olajuwon— and they most definitely still had the great Houston Rockets fans.

made his mark by adding one last important piece. The Rockets acquired veteran Mario Elie. At 6'5", the versatile Elie was known

The Best is yet to Come
In 1993-94, Hakeem appeared in 80 games and averaged 27 points, 12 rebounds, and more than three blocks per game.

On November 5, 1993, the Rockets opened up the 1993-94 season at home against the New Jersey Nets. Olajuwon had a ridiculous game, finishing with 24 points, 19 rebounds, six assists, and five blocked shots. Fans were used to these kinds of numbers from "Hakeem the Dream." However, other players contributed as well. Otis Thorpe had 15 points and 10 rebounds, while Robert Horry (18 points), Vernon Maxwell (16 points), and Kenny Smith (nine points) led a balanced attack. The end result was a Rockets blowout, 110-88. It was only one game, so it didn't mean anything. Or did it? This was a new season, and there was a reason for optimism. Something big was on the horizon, and this was only the beginning.

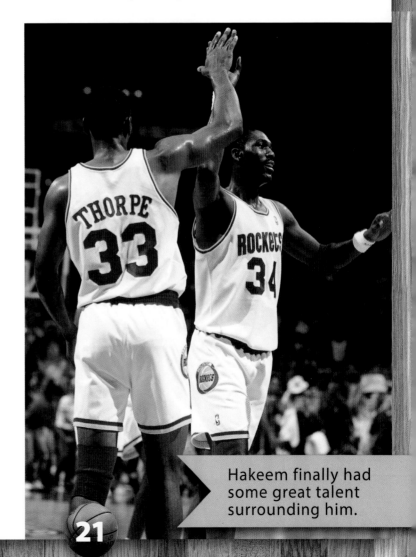

Hakeem finally had some great talent surrounding him.

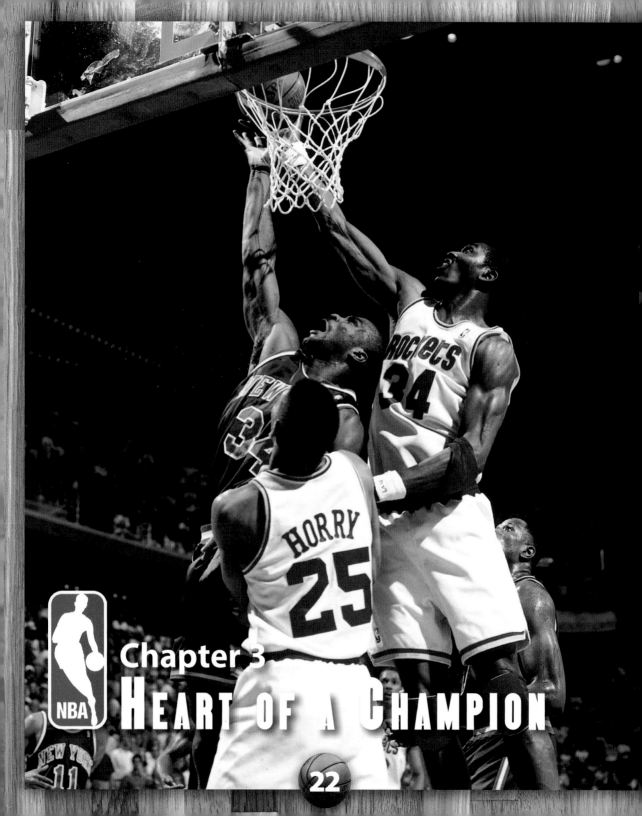

Chapter 3
HEART OF A CHAMPION

After beating the Nets in the opening game of the 1993-94 season, the Rockets kept on winning. Things were clicking for this talented and athletic team. Although this was a new Rockets team, one thing had not changed: Hakeem Olajuwon was still the center of attention. He was the one player who delivered night in and night out. At age 31, the perennial All-Star was having his greatest season ever.

With Olajuwon leading the way, the Rockets entered the 1994 play-offs brimming with confidence. After easily dispatching the Portland Trail Blazers in the opening round, they faced a stiff test in the semifinals of the Western Conference. Their

Charles Barkley and the Phoenix Suns presented a huge challenge for the Rockets.

opponents were the Phoenix Suns, led by a star-studded cast that included Charles Barkley and Danny Ainge.

After the Rockets lost the first two games of the series—at home—things looked very bad. But the Rockets showed great resolve, bouncing back and winning both games in Phoenix. The tone of the series had changed completely. By the time it was over, the Rockets had won in seven games—becoming only the second team in NBA history to win a series after losing the first two games at home.

All of a sudden, the Rockets were on a roll. After the historic win over Phoenix, they had no trouble with the Utah Jazz in the conference finals. They won that series four games to one. Finally, eight long years after the Twin Towers had led Houston to the NBA Finals, the Rockets had made it back. It wasn't going to be easy, though. Their opponents were the tough and rugged New York Knicks, led by Patrick Ewing.

The 1994 NBA Finals was an exciting and hard-fought seven-game series. Among the highlights was one of the greatest defensive plays in NBA history. Game 6 was

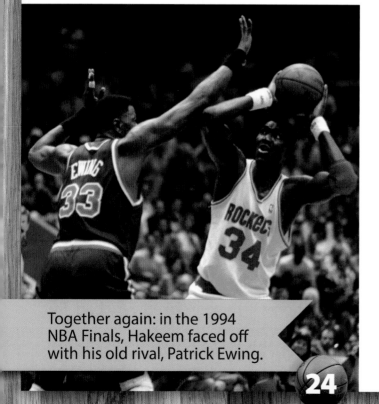

Together again: in the 1994 NBA Finals, Hakeem faced off with his old rival, Patrick Ewing.

played at the Summit in Houston, with the Knicks leading the series three games to two.

With only seven seconds to go in the game, the Rockets were up 86-84. However, the Knicks had the ball. After a time-out, the crowd nervously looked on as the Knicks inbounded the ball to their fiery guard John Starks above the three-point line.

The game, and the championship, came down to this showdown between John Starks and Hakeem.

All of a sudden, Patrick Ewing moved into the action, setting a giant pick which erased Vernon Maxwell. Dribbling toward the sideline, Starks—a clutch three-point specialist—knew exactly what he wanted to do: bury the Rockets once and for all. A three-pointer would not only win the game, it would win the championship!

Meanwhile, Olajuwon, who was guarding Ewing, understood what he had to do. He chased after Starks and leapt into the air, summoning the coordination and skill that had made him a great goalie in soccer. The crowd was on its feet. As Starks released the championship-winning attempt, Olajuwon managed to get a finger on it. He blocked the shot! The crowd went crazy as the clock expired. Olajuwon's heroics had saved the day, and the entire season.

After the dramatic conclusion to Game 6, nothing could stop the Rockets. Led by Olajuwon's 25 points, 10 rebounds, seven assists, and three blocks, they won a tough and well-deserved Game 7 by a score of 90-84. As for "Hakeem the Dream," it was a worthy ending to a season for the ages. He had won the regular-season MVP award, the DPOY (defensive player of the year)

The Rockets celebrate after being given the championship trophy.

award, and the Finals MVP award. He is the only player in NBA history who has accomplished that incredible feat. But he didn't care about the awards or the recognition. All he cared about was that his 10-year journey was complete. The Rockets were *finally* NBA champs!

In 1995, the city of Houston was still celebrating. Being known as the *world champion* Houston Rockets had a nice ring to it. However, people wondered how the Rockets would respond to being the champions. Would they be complacent, satisfied with finally winning it all? Or would they come back strong and try to repeat?

By the All-Star break, the Rockets were only 29-17…not a great record by the standards of defending NBA champions. They were looking vulnerable, so management stepped in and made a huge trade. The Rockets sent Otis Thorpe to the Portland Trail Blazers in exchange for Clyde Drexler. This was a joyous homecoming for the 6'7" Drexler, who was born and raised in Houston. It was also a reunion with Hakeem Olajuwon, the two most famous members of the high-flying and exciting Houston Cougars, who had reached the NCAA title game in both 1983 and 1984.

When the 1995 NBA playoffs began, many people had doubts about the Rockets. They had finished the season with a record of only 47-

Houston's Proud Son

Clyde Drexler's resume: NBA champion, Olympic gold medalist, 10-time All-Star, Hall of Famer.

Squaring off against the Suns once again, the Rockets had a new weapon—the high-flying Clyde "The Glide" Drexler.

poised to knock off the defending champions.

After defeating the Utah Jazz in a tough first-round series, the Rockets were matched up—once again—with the powerful Phoenix Suns. Just like the previous year, they fell behind two games to none. Even though the Rockets took Game 3, the Suns came back strong to win Game 4. Heading back to Phoenix, the Rockets were in a 3-1 hole. They had escaped during the previous season, but this time it seemed like there was no way out.

People had been doubting Houston all year long. Each time, the Rockets proved why they were the

35, and were entering the playoffs as the sixth seed. There were many strong teams that seemed to be

Long Odds
History was against the Rockets in the 1995 playoffs. No team had ever won the championship as a sixth seed.

defending champions. Giving it all they had, they fought back and won two games in a row, tying the series at three-all. Game 7 would be for all the marbles. Unfortunately, it was in Phoenix.

Game 7 was a fierce contest, with both teams fighting for every possession. When the Rockets found themselves down 114-112 with only seconds left, they needed a hero. They found one in "Super Mario".

Down by two points, 114-112, Kenny Smith brought the ball up the floor under duress from the Suns. He passed it to Robert Horry just beyond the midcourt line. Horry took one dribble and made a dangerous crosscourt pass to Mario Elie, who was open deep in the corner. Without hesitation, Elie took the shot. Nothing but net, game over, just like that! In a stunner, the Rockets had once again eliminated the Phoenix Suns in the semifinals of the Western Conference playoffs.

The Rockets were on a roll. After

"Super Mario" was a super clutch three-point shooter, as the Suns found out!

defeating the San Antonio Spurs in the Western Conference Finals, they marched into the NBA Finals against Shaquille O'Neal and the Orlando Magic. Once again, with their incredibly balanced attack, they found another hero. In Game 1, down by three points with less than two seconds to go, Kenny Smith hit a clutch three-pointer to send the game into overtime. Then, in overtime, the ever-reliable Hakeem Olajuwon provided his own heroics. With less than one second to go in overtime and the score tied 118-all, Olajuwon tipped in a Clyde Drexler miss, giving the game to the Rockets, 120-118.

The Magic weren't able to recover from their Game 1 loss, as the Rockets steam-rolled past them in four straight games. The entire city of Houston was delirious with joy as the Rockets closed out the series on their home floor, at the Summit in Houston. The Rockets had repeated as champions!

Drexler connects on a 20-footer in Game 3 of the 1995 NBA Finals.

It hadn't been easy, but the Rockets had never stop believing in themselves. Even when times had been difficult, they had pulled together. Their inspirational leader—Coach Rudy Tomjanovich—spoke to the crowd after the final game. His heartfelt words summed up the entire year. In fact, they were symbolic of the great Hakeem Olajuwon teams of the 1990s.

To the roar of the crowd, Coach Tomjanovich simply said: "I have one thing to say to those non-believers. Don't *ever* underestimate the heart of a champion."

After his inspirational speech to the crowd, Coach Tomjanovich celebrates with the great Hakeem Olajuwon.

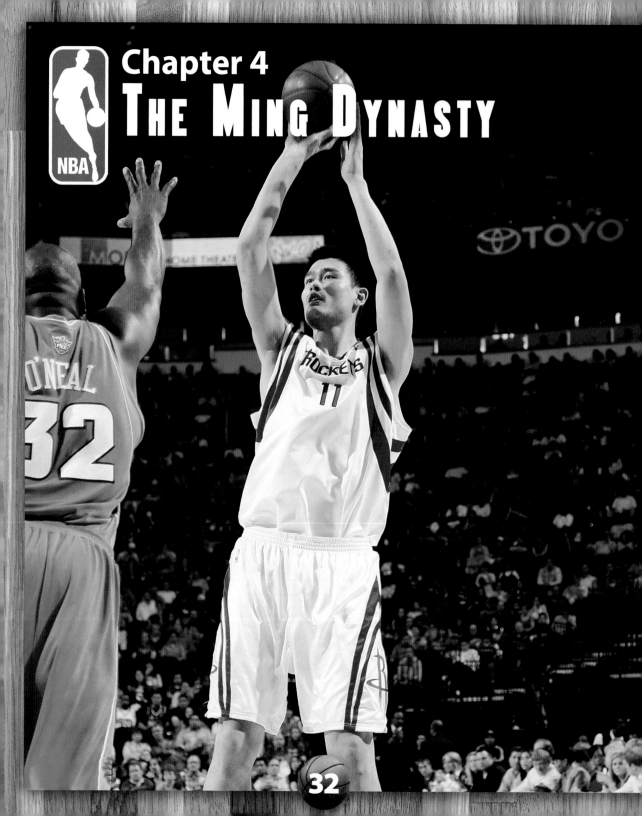

Chapter 4
THE MING DYNASTY

The date was June 27, 2002. This was a very important and exciting day for the country of China. Practically every TV set was on, tuned in to the 2002 NBA draft. It was taking place in New York on June 26. (China is 13 hours ahead of New York, so when the draft was taking place at 7:30 PM, it was 8:30 AM the following morning in China). The Houston Rockets had the number one pick in the draft. It had come about as the result of a very difficult season in which they had finished with a record of 28-54. Nobody was particularly surprised that the Rockets had struggled in the 2001-02 season. That's because it was their first year without Hakeem Olajuwon.

In the summer of 2001, after 17 memorable years with the organization, Olajuwon felt that it was time to move on. Respecting the wishes of their great star, the Rockets

One bright spot in the 2001-02 season was Stevie Francis. He was so valued that his nickname was "Stevie Franchise."

had traded him to the Toronto Raptors. Without question, it was the turning of a page. Even though the Rockets suffered without him, there was one upside: they had won the lottery and once again found themselves with the number one pick in the draft.

The Houston Rockets always had a tradition of bringing in Hall of Fame big men. It started with Moses Malone, and then there was Ralph Sampson. Of course, when Hakeem Olajuwon came along, it resulted in two spectacular championships. The question now: Where in the world could Houston find a suitable replacement for a Hall of Fame center like "Hakeem the Dream?"

Basketball fans in China knew

Coach Tomjanovich and all Rockets fans cherished Hakeem Olajuwon. Replacing him wouldn't be easy.

the answer to that question. So did the Houston Rockets! They were all well aware of a young giant named Yao Ming, who had been developing his basketball skills for many years in China.

Some NBA fans may not know that basketball has always been a very popular sport in China. As a matter fact, it caught on there very soon after Dr. James Naismith introduced it to the United States. There were many excellent Chinese players, and it was only a matter of time before the NBA would take notice. That happened in 1999, when the Dallas Mavericks drafted Wang Zhizhi in the second round. That opened the door for Chinese players to come to the United States.

By the time Yao Ming was only 10 years old, he was already well over five feet tall. Within a couple of years, he was practicing basketball several hours a day. It took time, but he developed into an unstoppable player. When he reached his final season in China, he was averaging 32 points and almost 20 rebounds per game. Meanwhile, he had continued to grow…and grow…and grow. Yao ended up standing an amazing 7'6"!

Commissioner David Stern stepped up to the podium to announce the first selection in the 2002 draft. An entire country far away from New York watched with anticipation. Mr. Stern finally spoke

Good Genes
Maybe it wasn't such a surprise that Yao ended up so tall: his father was 6'7", and his mother was over six feet tall!

"Guess what, Mom?" Yao talks on the phone moments after being drafted into the NBA.

very proud, and eager for the Ming Dynasty to begin in Houston. Fans in Houston were just as excited. They knew that it would take a lot more than just Yao to turn the team around, but this was a giant step forward.

Yao did not disappoint. His impact was felt right away. The Rockets showed great improvement and increased their total number of wins by 15 over the previous season. A couple of years later, they acquired high-flying guard Tracy McGrady from the Orlando Magic. There was a lot of excitement in Houston as the Rockets, led by Yao and McGrady, won 51 games in the 2004-05 regular season. They went into the 2005 postseason with confidence.

The Rockets had a very tough

the words they were waiting to hear: "With the first pick in the 2002 draft, the Houston Rockets select Yao Ming from Shanghai, China, and the Shanghai Sharks."

Many people in China let out a loud cheer. Most of them were beaming with pride. They were all first-round matchup. They had to go head-to-head with their intrastate rivals, the Dallas Mavericks. Things looked very good when the Rockets, led by McGrady and Yao, won the first two games. However, Game 3 saw the momentum in the series shift completely. The Rockets, playing at home at Toyota Center, went into the fourth quarter with a lead, 83-78. Unfortunately, in this pivotal game, the Mavericks came back, led by their super-star Dirk Nowitzki. In the end, the Mavericks squeaked it out by a score of 106-102. The tide had turned, and the Mavericks would go on to win the series in seven tough games.

The Rockets were used to dealing with adversity, so they

prepared to come back strong the following year. Unfortunately, as Rockets fans know very well, the injury bug would bite and change the course of history. Over the next three years, both Yao and McGrady

Rockets superstars Yao Ming and Tracy McGrady.

When Yao was healthy, nobody—not even the great Shaq—could stop him.

constantly missed a lot of action. This prevented the Rockets from finding the cohesion needed to advance far into the playoffs.

In the end, Yao's time as an NBA player—and as a Houston Rocket— was too short. However, his eight years in Houston left a very deep impression that will be felt for years to come. Attendance exploded in Houston, and people across the world (particularly in Asia) watched him on television. According to Kobe Bryant, Yao greatly influenced young people in China, "to believe that it's possible to achieve the dream of being an NBA player."

It's true that a lot of Yao's impact extended far beyond the basketball court. People will never forget his good humor, his warm smile, and his humanitarian efforts (such as donating $2 million after a devastating earthquake struck in a province of China in 2008).

Even as he battled injuries, Yao never lost his desire to play, or his love of the game. And when he was healthy enough to play, he was practically impossible to guard. Yao had a feathery shooting touch and could score inside and out. Over his eight years, he averaged 19 points and nine rebounds.

For people all across China—and around the world—Yao Ming was a hero. He defined an entire generation of basketball players. Yao was selected to the NBA All-Star team every single year of his career. That was a testament to his skill on the court – and his immense popularity off it.

Yao Ming is a humanitarian. Here he is pictured at an event to raise money for charity.

On October 27, 2012, the Houston Rockets were feeling optimistic about the state of their franchise. As they prepared for the new season, things were looking good. They had completed a successful preseason, winning five out of seven games. The roster was stocked with good young players. One of them was Chandler Parsons, a second-year player with tremendous upside. After leading the University of Florida Gators to the Elite Eight of the 2011 NCAA tournament, Houston had selected Parsons in the second round of the NBA draft. He didn't disappoint, earning a selection to the NBA All-Rookie Second Team in 2012.

Chandler Parsons goes strong to the hoop and scores.

Some new faces had joined Parsons over the summer. In fact, the Rockets had enjoyed a very productive off-season. On July 18, "Linsanity" had exploded in the city of Houston as Jeremy Lin put his signature on a three-year, $25 million deal.

Jeremy had become an overnight sensation just six months earlier with the New York Knicks. His meteoric rise in New York had been completely unexpected. As a matter fact, when the Knicks acquired him on December 27, 2011, his future was so uncertain that he didn't even bother to rent an apartment! Instead, he usually just slept on the couch at his brother's apartment. Another time, one of his Knicks teammates, Landry Fields, let Jeremy crash at his place.

But it didn't take long for things to change. On February 10, 2012, the star-studded Los Angeles Lakers arrived in New York to take on the Knicks. Madison Square Garden was packed, as it always is when a player like Kobe Bryant comes to town. Kobe didn't disappoint, scoring 34 points. Easy win for Lakers, right? It probably would have been, except that Kobe was outscored by... Jeremy Lin! The 22-year-old guard poured in an incredible 38 points,

Jeremy Lin scores on a beautiful driving layup.

leading the Knicks to a 92-85 win over the Lakers.

Suddenly, everybody took notice. The only thing people wanted to talk about was Jeremy Lin. He was named the Eastern conference Player of the Week. He appeared on the cover of Sports Illustrated—two weeks in a row! "Linsanity" was everywhere.

By the end of the season, Jeremy Lin was a worldwide figure. Everyone knew the story of this friendly, determined young man of Asian-American descent. There was only one question remaining for this

Jeremy Lin signs the contract that officially makes him a Houston Rocket.

restricted free agent—would his NBA career continue in New York, or could another team find a way to make him switch jerseys?

Gym Rat

Jeremy Lin is a true "gym rat"—someone who spends all his time in the gym trying to become a better player.

Enter the Houston Rockets. At this particular time, they were a team in rebuilding mode. They had lured Omer Asik away from the Chicago Bulls. The seven-footer from Turkey hadn't gotten a lot of playing time in Chicago because he was stuck behind terrific players like Joakim Noah and Carlos Boozer. Now, by signing Jeremy Lin, it was clear that the Rockets were moving in a very positive direction. However, they still needed a superstar-caliber scorer and playmaker. Every team needs a superstar that can be the face of the franchise. On October 27, 2012, the Rockets landed a spectacular young player who would not only be the face of the franchise—you might say he would be the "beard" of the franchise!

The huge trade took place between Houston and Oklahoma City. It sent shock waves through the NBA. The Thunder was a dynamic team that had reached the NBA Finals in 2012. They seemed poised to take the next step and become champions. However, they had committed a ton of money to their two main superstars, Kevin Durant and Russell Westbrook. They were worried about losing another of their young stars, James Harden, who was an upcoming free agent. So they agreed to trade Harden to the Rockets, a trade that included six players and three draft picks. As one newspaper reported, "The 'beard' has landed in Houston."

Most James Harden fans knew exactly what that headline meant. Harden had been in the league for only three years and had improved his scoring every season. In the 2011-12 campaign, he had averaged 16 points a game and captured the NBA's Sixth Man of the Year award.

He was the second youngest player to ever claim that honor. Everyone knew that James Harden was a rising superstar.

However, Harden had become more famous for his unique beard than his tremendous play on the court. According to most accounts, he had not shaved since entering

James Harden soars to the hoop in a game against the San Antonio Spurs.

James Harden elevates over Tristan Thompson of the Cavs and gets off his beautiful jumper.

opposing players definitely feared the beard (or at least the player who was wearing it).

In his first season as the new leader of the Rockets, James Harden exceeded even the loftiest expectations. It didn't take long to show fans what they had to look forward to. In the season opener against Detroit, Harden poured in an incredible 37 points and dished out 12 assists to lead his new team to an easy 105-96 win.

That was only the beginning. The 6'5" lefty would enjoy a remarkable season packed with highlights. He even had the chance to show his old team just how much they missed

the NBA more than three years earlier! His huge and bushy beard was an ongoing topic of conversation on the Internet and many other places. "Fear the Beard" had become a slogan. One thing was certain—

him. On February 20, 2013, Harden lit up the Oklahoma City Thunder with 46 brilliant points, helping the Rockets score the upset, 122-119. That performance had come on the heels of his first-ever triple-double, which he had accomplished earlier in February against the Charlotte Bobcats.

By the time the regular season had come to a close, James Harden had averaged 26 points, five rebounds, and five assists. Not surprisingly, he was selected to the All-Star game for the first time in his career. More importantly, along with Jeremy Lin, Chandler

Parsons, Omer Asik, and the rest of his talented teammates, he had led

James Harden is not only a uniquely skilled basketball player, but he's also a great leader.

the Rockets back to the playoffs for the first time in three years.

The city of Houston was thrilled and captivated by Harden, and by an entirely reshaped roster. The Rockets had a great coach in Hall of Famer Kevin McHale. With an offense that would be spearheaded by a backcourt of James Harden and Jeremy Lin, the Rockets were young, exciting, and hungry. Hopefully they will travel down the path of greatness very soon, make an impact in the playoffs, and then—once again— compete for the NBA championship!

With James Harden and Jeremy Lin leading the charge, Rockets fans have a lot to smile about.